Still Love

Advance Praise for This Book

Like the Irish playwrights including Sean O'Casey and Brian Friel who observed every nuance of daily life and transformed them into art, Jack Powers observes the living and the dying of everyone around him and makes memorable sonnets from what he sees. With intelligence, wit, and most of all compassion, these love poems that span the seven kinds of love (according to the ancient Greeks) are full of sentiment without being sentimental. Nothing is off limits. From the heartbreaking demise caused by dementia to the story of a nun who confesses to an abortion, Powers manages to write a book in which the seriousness of Victor Frankl and the levity of Monty Python exist in harmony and even feel inevitable. Powers is at the height of his poetic powers when he writes about love and death. "I don't spend much time visiting parents' graves./ What's gone is gone and I've got nothing to say/ to the dead." Powers may not have anything to say to the dead but he has a lot to say about them. And how they inhabit and teach the living. The entire book is a *memento mori* and these poems not only remind us that we are going to die but teach us how to live.

    — Jennifer Franklin, *If Some God Shakes Your House* (Four Way Books.

2003)

Jack Powers' five-part collection, *Still Love,* considers the changing nature of love as we age. With each poignant portrayal of deep love, we not only see into the author's life, but into our own. Powers demonstrates that it's important to be able to say of those we love, "I still see you" ("A Nod to the Master"), even when they are gone. His training as an artist is apparent in the rich images: "Even the boy knows/ not to speak, just feel the surf and watch the sky turn purple then black" ("Keeper"). Or "Why stop at fifty words for *snow* or *love*? Coin a word each time/ they fall, whitening weathered fields, making the world new" ("Every Snowflake"). These poems teach us that "you must embrace your life"—however much of it we have left—but also that embracing it requires us to slow down long enough to see what our world is made of. This is love poetry to his wife and family, and to the world.

— Laurel S. Peterson, author of *Daughter of Sky*

Everybody has taken their chances at love and fidelity in Jack Powers' endearing second collection, *Still Love.* Many are housed in his sonnets of modern architecture. (See the tiny-house half-sonnet about how to hold on while surgically removing a heart.) His characters may be discovering more about each other, encouraging new liaisons at the senior memory center, even divorcing in their nineties. This is a book about enduring and declining, engaging and resisting, persevering. It includes narratives about the poet as a young man in the company of the old people he'd "always liked [but] never wanted to be," as well as about the present-day retiree fashioning poems about the poems we've just read. A good Powers poem is one that laughs at itself—and at you—while paying close attention to shifts in diction and memory, and to the traps of longevity and belief, but most of all to the abundance and wonder of life.

— Amy Holman, *Wrens Fly Through This Opened Window*

Still Love

Poems

Jack Powers

Golden Antelope Press
715 E. McPherson
Kirksville, Missouri 63501
2023

ISBN: 978-1-952232-75-6

Library of Congress Control Number: 2023930527

Published by:
Golden Antelope Press
715 E. McPherson
Kirksville, Missouri 63501

Available at:
Golden Antelope Press
715 E. McPherson
Kirksville, Missouri, 63501
Phone: (660) 229-2997
http://www.goldenantelope.com
Email: ndelmoni@gmail.com

Author's Note

After 40 years of teaching, I wanted to write every day and live my last stretch with grace and good humor. I've been very fortunate and enjoyed many identities: wise-ass Jack, artist Jack, dad Jack, teacher Jack. Could I pull off one more meaningful transition? To manage this three-quarter-life crisis, I turned to those around me for forewarnings and inspiration. My older siblings had not yet retired; my grandfathers died young; my grandmothers hung on as they dwindled away to nothing; my parents had some good years, but their slow declines into dementia and Parkinson's-like withdrawal left the biggest impression. I needed to look elsewhere. The sonnet seemed the perfect vessel to capture my observations and to keep me from wandering, while still requiring a turn or two to push me toward surprise or insight. Although I didn't follow my own directions (sonnets became sonnet-ish, outward-focused soon turned inward, and last acts mixed with firsts and middles), I kept my gaze on people who found or didn't find meaning, who aged or didn't age gracefully. I like to think I've learned something.

* Source for each found poem is cited below the poem. Other citations are in the End Notes.

Contents

Unruly Love   **42**

Noble Suffering   **62**

Surrender 75

End Notes 87

Acknowledgements 91

Praise for *Everybody's Vaguely Familiar* 93

Last Act

Last Act

I laughed with my doctor at his patient who said,
I want you to be my last doctor, imagining him checking that
off his list of last barber, last mailman, last mechanic –
a dark laugh that ended in a shared sigh at his audacity.
And ours. At 65, I've started thinking about my last dog,
my last house. I figure I have ten good years left
before the marbles go. Time enough if used well
for one last act. One new start. But no time to lollygag.

My yoga teacher says, *Breathe. Just be.*
My writing teacher says, *Cut 'lollygag.'* Instead I look up
synonyms and linger in the *shilly-shally* of now,
the *dawdle, crawl,* the *tarry, drag* and *lag,*
the assonance of *last act,* of sound slowing time, laughing
at *marbles* and *audacity,* of planning a *last* anything.

Losing Things

My wife worried what we'd do when we retired.
So far we're spending it looking for things:
keys, coats, glasses. Sometimes they're on our heads
Or in our hands. Sometimes on an odd shelf.
At first it's irritating, then a challenge.
I walk the house, looking through my wife's eyes
from breakfast table to bathroom, in closets, in couches.
Or think like a wallet or phone. Where would I hide?

As my father's dementia deepened, he lost his edge,
his quick sarcasm. Or maybe he just forgave us,
released the resentments, forgot the ways we'd let him down
and he became, if not a hugger, a ready smiler, a back patter, a fan.

Once I found a birthday card drawn by my son at two. I looked like
a smiling potato. When dementia comes, I hope it's the forgiving kind.

Holding On

A couple in their nineties announce they're getting divorced. *Why now?*
they're asked. *We wanted to wait until the children had died.* If children
follow romance, what follows children? I study old neighbors for clues.

Sally sits on our stonewall when her hip acts up on walks. Her husband, Phil,
sits beside her and lets her do the talking. *What's your name again?* she asks me.
They hold hands like seventh graders. *Our children are all grown and gone.*

Gil and Cindy sit outside when it's warm. He talks openly about her dementia.
When it's cold, she sneaks out of the house and walks. *She doesn't go far,*
Gil says. *I keep an eye on her from the window. She says she's going home.*

The Porters kept the house like a museum of knickknacks and photographs.
It smelled like 1962, the year Ben coached the football team to the State title.
He drove the old pick-up. Liz made lunch. She died three days after Ben.

Each anniversary, a couple in their nineties sky dives using one chute.
Asked the secret of their longevity, they said, *Make sure you go together.*

A Little Red

Aunt Pauline started painting in her sixties,
little watercolors of beach scenes and roses,
matted and framed on her kitchen walls.
Her football-coach husband seemed mystified
by her sudden secret life. Each Tuesday
she packed her paints and set off for class
with 80-something Mitch Mendelson,
the watercolor king of Englewood, New Jersey.
Put a little red, he'd say, *in each painting*,
and she'd comply. Each week a new picture
was framed and hung, soon covering
the dining room, the living room, even
the basement man cave—a little red in each.
At Mitch's funeral, she put a red ribbon in his casket.

How to Hold a Heart

Slide your hand behind the heart
until you can feel your knuckles graze
the smooth pericardial sac encasing it.
Once the organ is centered in your palm, lift up.

Always cradle it in two hands. Squeeze
the pinkie sides of your palms together, overlapping

your fingers as if you are scooping up water to drink.

FOUND POEM SOURCE: "Tip: How to Hold a Heart." Malia Wollan, *New York Times*, Jan. 8, 2016.

On Turning 61

For Katie

Consider this as your heart beats so steady for so long you've forgotten
you're always counting to its steady *bumpbumpbump.* Listen to your lungs
swell and ease beneath your breast, companions from the moment
you popped into this world. You've known the fear,
the unfairness, the stranger in the mirror, the thickened tongue,
the distance from yourself and everyone, yet now you sit
at this table, your hale and good husband intent at his own good work,
your children off composing babies and song—oh, that grandchild grows so fast!

And here in this little pond where you spend your days, you are famous,
on a first-name basis with the only world that matters right now
as you quarter your avocado. Could you be any richer in this moment,
carving out its hard seed, peeling away its dark skin, dicing cubes,

green-yellow just-ripe meat, before dropping it on your greens,
and stealing a bite off the knife's edge?

Next

My father loved his house, framing pictures
on Christmas cards, often standing in the driveway
shadowed by our giant oak, admiring it like his newborn.
Long before the stroke, he'd pause while raking leaves
or mowing the lawn and just stare at the house—an ordinary house,
as far as I could tell. He'd laugh when caught in that absent gaze.
I read those photos now like ancient texts: lines of clapboard,
shutters like brackets—could the windows crack the code?

He built it, not with his hands, but with his sweat,
his capital squirreled away for the next Great Depression
but unearthed for this one clear monument to how far
he'd come from rented claptraps in Springfield, Mass.

I'm just guessing. He told us nothing and we didn't ask.
Was he already slipping? Was I too dense to see?

*****

I've always liked old people
—growing up with two grandmothers
didn't leave much choice. There was nothing
noble about it: Nanny snuck me cigarettes
and Granny laughed at my teasing
—making her speak CB language or say *Fart*.
We killed a lot of time together—me waiting
for life to start and them for it to end.

Dad's slide into dementia somehow softened him
and my mother's slow decline was like Granny redux.
I chat with older neighbors now, learn how things have changed
and how they made it through, catching their smiles

at my futile pursuit of a greener lawn or a cooler mailbox.
I've always loved old people—just never wanted to be one.

*****

After Nanny and Granny died, my father knew he was next.
With his work and children gone, the house
was the one solid thing he could take credit for. Is that it?
Once the hubbub of living quiets, where will I cast my gaze?

I'm the second son, but his clone. Determined to be his opposite,
but foiled. At his funeral, old friends dropped off in front
crawled out of backseats like they were climbing out of caskets,
steadying themselves on the pavement with walkers or canes.

I watched their startled faces when they looked up as I,
now silver-haired like my dad, same blue eyes, short nose,
height and bearing, greeted them at the curb. Some wobbled
and I worried they'd go down. I caught one or two by the elbow.

Your Father... they said. *You look... I thought...*
Yes, I said, *like twins*, now knowing I was next.

*****

As the oldest son, Donny gave the eulogy
and told a story about his friend Dave Doran
driving by the house in his electrician's truck
and seeing my father in the driveway, staring
at the gutters. Or maybe the flagstone steps?

When he returned an hour or so later,
service call complete, he found Dad still gazing.

Donny told it as one more mysterious Dad story,
but the church rang with laughter of old friends
who knew something we didn't. Outside the church,

we shook their hands wanting to ask, but they were all
so sorry and the funeral seemed to sap them so.

They each turned, fell into their back seats
pressed their faces to the windows and waved goodbye.

Still Love

Keeper

A fisherman stands bow-legged in shallow surf, water to his ankles.
Beside him stands his miniature—right down to the blue cap.
                                                    The sun flares
yellow above trees already dark with night. House lights flicker on one by one.
The fishermen are silent.
                    Even the surf seems to have quieted its steady breath.
Seagulls ride drafts overhead without a caw and a school of fluke separates
around the wiggling bait in the shape of two hands praying.

Father and son gaze at the water rippling with orange sky, neither willing
to let the day end.
                    On the shore, their basket shows a meager haul: a flounder,
two Blackfish just past the legal limit—none of the Blues, the father'd described
in bedtime stories once leaping out of the Sound almost jumping into his boat.

But this moment—close enough to hear each other breathing with the surf
and the breeze, their lines holding the pink of the clouds, imagined Blues
circling out beyond their casts—is enough.
                            Even the boy knows
not to speak, just feel the surf and watch the sky turn purple then black.

Still Love

I was her rebellion. Ben drinks his beer.
And she was my shot at normalcy.

We lasted ten years. He sighs, sips again.
She got over rebelling, and I guess

I couldn't be normal. His smile suggests
that last part is a joke or at least a funny

truth. But his story, listing all the moves
and arguments, leaves out those moments

when it worked or they believed it would
and laughed or made love. It's the end he recalls

when she told their therapist, *Don't listen to him,
He's evil.* Yet she got him to a doctor

when he said, *I just want to dive in the ocean
and keep swimming.* Wasn't that still love?

Where Was Your Mother?

Hors d'oeuvres, I said and placed a bowl of grapes on the table.
Mom, Ellen, and Granny must have looked at me strange,
but I was focused on making dinner. *Cheeseburgers*
on cinnamon-and-sugar-coated English muffins, I narrated
as I worked Mom's electric grill. Why did I feel so confident
when the friends I'd smoked angel dust with had all freaked out?

I focused on getting a little char on the burgers
while keeping the middle pink, timing the muffins browning
in our little toaster, slicing the tomato. As my friends
wandered Guy's yard crying or lay on his living room floor
mumbling at their hands, I decided I needed to ride home
and cook dinner. Dad was away so I wouldn't get his
are-you-stoned-again? look and Mom could probably
use a break. And who wouldn't love grapes and burgers?

I centered the burgers on muffins and tomatoes on beds of iceberg,
and presented each plate with a silent *Voila!* then sat beside them
and dug in, *Mmm*-ing and saying *Delicious, right?* It was.
Twenty-five years later, at our group-fortieth birthday party,
Dan's wife, Michelle, kept interrupting our crazy stories
with *Where was your mother?* Most of the time Mom was busy
trying to live her own life and following the *Don't ask,*
Don't tell policy that kept us from arguing all the time.

But for the bowl-of-grapes dinner, she was sitting to my left.
Did she look at her wild-eyed teen son, hair in a frizzy ponytail
and think, *Should I call someone?* Granny laughed at my *Mmms*,
ate, probably thinking I'd be a chef instead of the priest she'd hoped for.
Ellen was probably trying to divert attention from my cryptic babbling
and long silences. But Mom? She was a child of The Depression,
an adult of the Eisenhower years. The hippies and drugs of the sixties
were beyond her understanding. Or was I selling her short?

During my delinquent phase in seventh grade,
she used to save things up. *Can I sleep at Tommy's?*
I asked once on a car ride home. *I've been really good.*
What about, she asked, *trying to set Old Greenwich School on fire?*
We weren't—, I said. *It was just a little fire to burn the—*
We put it out, I said, remembering all the steam rising from our pee
that brought the fire trucks. Mom turned her eyes back to the road
with a little smile. She knew me pretty well.

I think I knew when my own kids were stoned,
though it could have been just the surliness of teen-hood.
Would I have interrupted a surprise dinner of grapes
and burgers to let them know I knew? After the plates
were scraped clean, I noticed the half-filled bowl.
The grapes are dessert, too, I said. *What symmetry!*

We each grabbed one, bit into the tart green skin.
I imagined simultaneous explosions of sweetness in our mouths.
We looked out the window at the yellow forsythia,
the squirrels playing in the giant oak, the tomatoes and corn
I'd planted in the garden—all lost in our own thoughts.
Where was my mother? Right beside me the whole time.

Every Snowflake

The Inuit do not have fifty words for snow, but the Greeks had eight words
for love: that familiar kind you pack in blocks and build into a home,
that flirty type that lures you to the window but doesn't stay, the practical

that treats a sprain or chills a beer, the friendly solid base
for the grip and glide of fellowship, that self-polished sort for ogling
your own reflection, that manic type that blinds you in a storm,

even that pristine-landscape kind that leaves your mouth agape. But
we talk only of the *sparkle in moonlight* kind, the *never touches ground* kind,
the *captured in lines and offered in cupped hands to a lover* kind.

But what of snow angels and snow globes and snow forts dug on snow days,
what of swirling snow in April dusting crocuses and daffodils, what
of snow squalls and avalanches and glittering snow on bowing branches?

Why stop at fifty words for snow or love? Coin a word each time
they fall, whitening weathered fields, making the world new.

Sisters

Connie used to be the quiet one when they came at Christmas.
While Tina told New York stories, punctuated by her boisterous laugh,
or tales about growing up in the Bronx across the hall from my mother,
Connie sat apart on the sofa. She'd nod or drift into her own thoughts.

Now Connie's the talker, her walker stashed by the wall. *I never watch,*
she claims, as the TV blares in front of us. *An old movie, maybe*
on—what's that channel? I read mostly. Behind her Tina's shaking her head.
At 95 and 92, they share a rent-controlled apartment near the Village.

We eat ham steak, unsalted mashed potatoes and apple sauce because
Connie's wheelchair can't navigate the rain. *Sister,* Tina says, *try the ham.*
You like ham. She cuts Connie's meat. *Sometimes,* Connie says,
I sneak out when Tina's not looking. Tina shakes her head again.

They stand in their doorway as we walk to the elevator—a picture
of saying goodbye: two white-haired sisters, hands waving in unison.

Glide and Grip

Tommy Carroll was the first to get his license, and we could pile fourteen guys
into his mom's Ford Country Squire if three of us sat on the lowered tailgate.

Suddenly the world expanded past Ada's Variety, out of bike range,
across town lines on long drives to anywhere, to nowhere.

We jammed half our ninth grade team into that car when playing football
just meant more time to savor both the glide and the grip of friendship.

Saturdays, we'd drive down 95 to play miniature golf or see a drive-in movie.
On the way back, sparks flew from the heels of our loafers scraping the highway.

Even on Christmas, I snuck out to see Tommy, Brian and Dave,
more like family than anyone sitting around that table.

Jostling and joking and shout-singing to the AM radio, time flew by faster
than Tommy could crank up that old wagon, even though he hit 90 once on a dare.

When we hit a bump, our butts would jump off the tailgate and we'd shout and
hold each other as we hurtled backwards, sparks rising from the dark road.

Flirts

Once Nanny settles in her pew, she searches the back rows
as she catches her breath. Down to ninety pounds, her fragile heart
made the walk down the aisle feel like a marathon. She'd layered on rouge
and bright red lipstick, slept in curlers to get some bounce back
in her dyed blonde hair.
     I don't even know his name, she whispers
as she pretends not to see him—still broad shouldered in his tailored pinstripes.
Under thick gray brows, he scans, then nods. She turns to face the altar.

After Mass, she waits at the curb in the April sun. He stops,
removes his fedora and, in a gravelly voice, asks, *How are you today?*
She blushes. *Fine,* she says, sticks her chin in the air. *And you?*
He smiles. *Very good.* He leans in closer. *Very good.*
         For a moment,
she becomes her twenty-something self, beguiling young Springfield suitors
on Sunday trips with the girls to Brigham's. Her eyes are blue as the sky!
He limps off, turns at the corner, puts two fingers to the brim of his hat.

Just Say It's a Miracle

But how does the sperm get to the egg? Zak asked.
He was seven. We were brushing our teeth.
I tried to give him the seven-year-old's answer.

He knew Anne and I were going to specialists
to give him and Erin a baby brother.
The penis, I said, *goes into the vagina.*

I'd started with mommies' tummies
and daddies' love, but each answer
led to a new question. *And sends the sperm*

swimming toward the egg. Zak nodded,
spit in the sink, seemed satisfied.
I turned to go. *You and Mom did that?* he asked.

I nodded sheepishly. *At the doctor's office?*
Anne would say I'd shared too much.

But I knew I'd said too little. What I'd described
could well have happened under fluorescent lights
with clinicians scribbling on clipboards

and paper rolled out to keep the bed clean
for the next subjects. I should have shared the years
of bad dates and disappointments, my gift of flowers

stolen from her neighbor, Anne's quick laugh, her eyes
and hips, the first stolen kisses, the fumbling
and sweating in cars, the moaning and giggling

and joy of finding each other, and the desperate need
to have a third despite miscarriages
and the indifferent universe. And the scheming

to get him and Erin asleep so we could try again,
shushing each other like teenagers so they didn't wake.

And later the leap of hope at the missed period
and Anne's rounding belly, the awe and joy
in my own chest and our laughter when

we called from the delivery room as we waited
and Zak, then eight, asked about contractions
and dilation. And the fear when Baby Will arrived,

with his cord wrapped around his neck
and the relief when it was clipped and uncoiled,
and he took his first sputtered breath.

Parenthood is full of regrets that drown out the moments
of indescribable joy like the wide-eyed look
on Zak's face when he first held Baby Will,

and twenty-five years later when he held his own Baby Zuri,
gobsmacked, babbling, stumbling to put it into words.

Rejoice in the Cat

After Christopher Smart

Writing about cats will cast me as crazy.
Smart's paean to God and Jeoffry was a prayer
penned in an asylum cell. So many women
I love say they fear becoming cat ladies. And
Broadway aside (or is it proof?), Eliot's cat
fetish is a cat box mystery to me. Still,

consider my cat George, every-day named,
servant to no one, seventeen, who shares my birthday,
thinning ragamuffin, begging to be lifted to his bowl.
He sits before me on the table licking white paws,
waiting for my scratch under his jaw, his chin,
settling into a soft purr, haunched, fur a little ragged.

He steps back, kneads, licks a paw absently.
I smile, reminded, it's not just about me.

Mgothger and Dgaughtger

When Mom dragged us out on errands, Mary sat up front and they chatted
in their secret language. Did she say *Jgohnnagie and Dgannagy?* I'd ask Danny,
but they'd moved on. We could never keep up. They were two best friends

out shopping while Danny, Ella and I fought in the back over window seats,
drawing lines to stake out territory. When Mary turned sixteen, their *Uga* lingo
was replaced by screaming about boys and curfews and the smell of alcohol,

rising to a crescendo when she moved in with her post-college boyfriend.
She was exiled: suddenly *Pgersagonaga non ggrataga.* We couldn't even
talk about her. When she left him, Mary was forgiven and invited home,

but instead she moved to Boston, keeping a cool distance. Once Mom
was alone, Mary started visiting on weekends. And when Mom stopped talking,
Mary spoke for her: *Mom doesn't want that* or *Mom wants you to...*

I'd returned to the back seat. And they'd circled back to *bgestaga frgiendsaga.*
Yes, yes, Mary murmured as she massaged Mom's feet or wiped Mom's chin.

A Nod to the Master

Zippy Stolfi distilled the head nod to its essence in seventh grade
from the moment he first appeared at the beach that summer:

chin lifted an eighth of an inch, dark brows tightened but not raised,
brown eyes saying *I see you*. What elegance and economy.

Sincere but not eager. Cool. Effortless. We couldn't respond in kind
so we slapped him five, said, *What's up?* shouted, *Zippeeee!*

We practiced at home in mirrors, never getting it quite right,
but learning the eyes and brow were key. I've been distracted since

by the high five, the clasped grip, the fist bump, the elbow tap, even
the garish *Yo, yo, yo,* but I always return to the simplicity of Zippy's nod.

When I heard he died of cancer, forty years after we'd last met,
I still felt the sharp stab of his loss, of a door closing on an era,

on a little known master who died too young. So I raise my chin to you,
one last nod, across this lifetime: Zippy, I still see you.

Unearthed

When Jim googled me, my picture appeared
above the bio of a Jack Powers
born 1827, soldier, gambler,
horseman, accused killer, outlaw.

You look good for 192,
Jim wrote. Now I contemplate my name-kin,
murdered and robbed by *vaqueros* in 1860,
now lying in a rocky grave.

How many other name-kins await mis-googles
to unearth their long-buried bones and bios?
Stone Soup poet Jack, Manhattan coach Jack,
actor Jack, all reborn from one flawed algorithm.

What do I owe all past and future Jacks?
Should I help Death Row Jack get his life back?

                    *****

Two weeks later a teacher emails me
for help with a poem by Stone Soup Jack.
I am the wrong Jack Powers, I reply,
but find him a YouTube reading, a fan blog,

thinking it's the least I can do for kin
and fellow poet. Though, I'd do the same
for car salesman Jack, truck mechanic Jack,
lying in graves with my name edged in stone.

The teacher emails me a thank you and says,
You may be the WRONG Jack Powers now but

be the RIGHT Jack Powers in the future.
If I take care of my name-kin, perhaps

after I ride off in that black Cadillac,
some future Jack will briefly snatch me back.

Old and New

All my best is dressing old words new,
Spending again what is already spent
from Sonnet LXXVI

In an age when everything's been said and done and felt,
when love's become cliché, expressed best by analogy—
like Adam and Eve, like Daisy and Jay, like Lucy and Desi—

when love has been defamed, demoted, deconstructed,
Hallmarked, simplified to swiping right,
                                                    when everything
is known and nothing is novel, can we still nod
at The Bard's conclusion, *For as the sun is daily new*
and old,/ so is my love still telling what is told?

And what of the two ninety-somethings strapped side-
by-side in wheelchairs, steered to their nursing-home table,
minds as soft as the carrots spooned by attendants
into their open mouths?
                                    They reach for each other.
He hooks a pinky into hers and she lifts her quivering,
purpled hand to pluck a white hair off his sleeve.

Lover/Loved

Must there always be lover and loved
spooner and spooned, hand and glove
why not equal parts of held and hold
tongue and groove, folded and fold

Must one always encircle the other
one absorb, one soak another
can age be blamed, is it gender
do genes assign tendee and tender

Or is loving an art that can be learned
accepting love a talent to develop
can one change from yearner to yearned
to both surround and be enveloped

And why is it when push comes to shove,
I choose to be the lover, not the loved?

Lover/Loved?

I choose to be the lover, not the loved
or am I just nursing bruises from the shove—
and-be-shoved jostle of our daily ties,
the hold and chafe that keep us equalized?

Tomorrow, might I say that I'm the latter?
A good night's sleep, a kiss, some morning chatter
and my wounded heart will grow warm and full,
love's tides abate and ease the push and pull?

> And when an old friend says, *We never fought,*
> After her husband's sudden split, I'm caught
> Between shock and sorrow. She never stopped
> to shake that vinegar to the top?

Sometimes it's selfishness that's saving us.
When they made nice, they should have made a fuss.

Bert and Kay

Bert always felt like a prop the way Kay fleshed out her stories
with *Bert said this. Bert did that*—long before I met him. When I'd call,
he was a deadpan voice on the phone: *Is Kay there?* Silence. *Yes.* More silence.

Can I speak to her? His ministry seemed to contradict Kay's devoted atheism
or maybe provided balance to the universe. He, always in black with white collar;
she, in English-teacher dress—always the smartest person in the room. And now

he opens the door, thanks me for coming and ushers me into the back room
where Kay sits in a stuffed chair with a view of the yard framed by a big window.
Jack has come to visit! says Bert, two levels too loud. *Well,* says Kay, *Hello, Jack.*

I only talk of the past—questions about her day or her grandchildren
make her stumble. Bert retires to his study. I wonder if he writes sermons still
for his congregation of one. She is most fluent about the yard: birds and maples,

the scurry of squirrels, leaves growing and falling. I think of her quoting Thoreau.
I run out of questions and listen as Kay listens to nature and Bert listens to God.

Provincetown, 2010

They think they've capped the BP oil leak, but I shudder
and worry only about myself—whether the oily mane
can wrap itself around the Keys and ride the Gulf Stream towards me,

black waves saddling up to random pelicans, and I wonder
about Cleopatra who I learned in a Philadelphia museum last week
had to marry her brother and maybe even her son

to ensure their line to the Gods and how just beneath the surface
of modern-day Alexandria Bay, they found the remnants of her temple:
two sphinx guarding the entrance, a priest bearing a jug, the garden

where Marc Antony took his life thinking Cleopatra was dead—
and I brush my teeth and start the day stretching my cramping shoulders,
crunching against gravity's inevitable pull and wonder

if I would kill myself if I heard Anne was dead. Still feeling the weight
in my morning stomach of two soft yellow eggs, grilled ham
and croissants, I suspect my appetite for the world is too great

to ever willingly leave it despite my claims each time
I return from my mother's mumbling haze. Even my joy
in my new ASICs, identical almost to the last pair

minus the stains and worn pinkie toe holes, is too great to leave—
so new their coming out party was a parade last night
down Commercial Street as they helped me find, I hope,

the right balance of friendliness and hetero-ness.
On the phone last night after listening to Anne's warranted whine
about sitting for two hours at the GW Bridge, I told her

that this is how rumors get started: some vacationing kids spot me
walking proudly—momentarily perhaps next to the well-muscled
Bette Midler impersonator—and word gets back

that I spend my summers in Provincetown dressed as a woman
singing show tunes in a husky falsetto—*I Will Survive* comes to mind—
a proud, sneakered, Caucasian, grey-haired Gloria Gaynor.

I understand now that she was right to tell me I was selfish to talk
of offing myself at 80 after watching my father's dementia slide.
The idea is not to leave a survivor but to go together somehow

not in a suicide pact or in some distraught reaction to the news
of the other's death (what if, like Antony, the messenger is wrong?)
No. We must go in sleep, maybe a night apart, so no one needs to wake

morning after morning in the bed alone after dreams like last night's
of shouting across a rocky chasm, her cupping her ear to hear me
before I'm in a car dropping down some hill steep as a pool slide,

before being jolted awake in this half-empty bed in the Carpe Diem
Guesthouse, imagining the impression of her shoulders and ass on the bed,
the dent her head would make in the wadded pillow. Tonight,

when I sit alone in some restaurant watching the gulls and fishing boats,
and surrounded by sunburned families and suntanned bachelors—
eating a big salad because survival is the key for now—

I'll wish I'd talked her into coming here with me so we could ride horses
along the beach, and remind ourselves to breathe in the salt air
(Breathe in and breathe out. Breathe in. Breathe out.)

Unflinching

> *I love to paint people who have been torn to shreds by the rat race*
> *–Alice Neel*

In her final painting, Alice Neel is eighty, nude, sitting on a blue striped chair,
paint brush in her right hand, painting rag in her left. Her body at an angle
accents her belly, the hunch in her back. Unflinching, despite breakdowns,
lost children, poverty, neglect, she painted what she saw in all its grotesque
beauty. *Look at all the furniture she has to carry,* Neel said about her first nude,
the heavy thighs, bulging stomach, and pendulous breasts. A diagonal line
divides the floor into orange and green. One foot rests in each.
But her head turns to us, glasses on, as if to say, *It's just a fact of life.*

Alice loved a wretch, her daughter-in-law said. *She loved the wretch*
in the hero and the hero in the wretch. She saw that in all of us.

Look closer. Her right toes are planted, heel raised, ready to rise again,
step to the easel, catch the slope of her shoulder in blue outline or the shadow
of the chair leg anchoring her in painted space. Her brush clutched like a sword,
her eyes say she *has a claim staked out; she is not for sale.* Hero. Wretch.

Found

It had been an act of courage to let herself love Howie,
knowing that they would not be able to do so for long,
and that one would inevitably watch the other decline.

In 2019, death moved more prominently into view.
Helen began hospice care last January after her kidneys failed,
but then she bounced back, noticeably more sedate than in past years.

On one visit, she did not recognize me at first. Then she said I needed a haircut.
Another time, a surprise: Helen was wearing three wedding rings.
For five years she had talked about wanting to marry Howie, but now,

not a word about it. *Helen,* I asked, *does that mean you are married?*
She smiled for the first time and held out her hand. *Correct, sir,* she said.
Close, anyway: commitment ceremony, just a few relatives.

She wore a pink dress with pearls around her neck
and an oxygen hose threaded under her nose.

FOUND POEM SOURCE: "She Is 96 and Does Not Fear Her Death. But Do Her
Children?" John Leland, *New York Times,* January 3, 2020

Where the Story Ends

From a distance he'd looked like a pile of logs fallen out of a truck, but why a red flag draped on the side? We'd just arrived in town, and knew no one. At two a.m. with temps in the teens, we shivered in front of the Forest Queen Hotel picturing some drunk plowing his pickup into the dark mess. At twenty feet, the pile took the shape of a body, a boy seventeen or so–a little younger than me—wearing only a red turtleneck against the icy night. I remember the Milky Way arching like a white stony river across the Colorado sky and mountains surrounding us on three sides: snow thick at the peaks.

I've tried to write this story for years, but couldn't capture how we told it again and again that winter: Tom embellishing until I almost couldn't recognize it, Fred telling it modestly in a barebones style, together improvising, trading off the solos. Forty-six years probably made other changes.

Is he dead? I asked feeling his cold forehead. *No, there's a pulse,* Tom said, two fingers at his windpipe. Barely. Fred and I each grabbed an arm and his shirt peeled off the frozen road with the *Shirritttt* sound of tape pulled off a package. Fred, still cut like a high school wrestler, started to lift him when the kid came to and started mumbling, said he lived in the grey house at the end of the street. He shook us off when we tried to help him walk and he began staggering toward the dead end. We followed.

My plan had been just to share a ride to Crested Butte with Tom, a friend of my brother's and Fred, a friend of Tom's, and hitch to Telluride to work in a mine and then head south to Guatemala in the spring. We'd come west to take a pause: Tom after college, Fred after a business gone sour, me after sophomore year. But as Tom's '65 Olds raced from Connecticut to Wisconsin to get Fred and then across the prairies and we peed in bottles and changed drivers by slithering over the seats, stopping only for gas and food, we'd become The [Tre]Mendous Brothers. Even had our own handshake.

The house at the end of the street looked grey but dark. We knocked. The kid started yelling, *Wake the fuck up!* We knocked again. Nothing. The kid kept yelling. He sounded delirious. I raised my hand to knock again when a porch light turned on behind us. An old man at the neighbor's door held a shotgun in his hand–his face in shadow. *You breaking into my sister's house?* he asked and laughed what I can only recall as a cackle. He wore a white t-shirt. He pumped the gun. *Not so loud now, are you?*

The kid started yelling. Tom said, *He lives here. We found him–* The man shouted, *Shut up!* Tom, always confident he could explain, said, *But sir–* That started the cackling again. *But sir,* the old man mimicked. We stepped back from the door. The kid resisted. We raised our hands in surrender, bracing for the blast. I tried again to pull the kid with us as we retreated. *No problem, sir,* I said. The kid stumbled backward, swearing. *Our mistake,* Fred said. *Damn right, it's your mistake!* the old man shouted.

When Fred died, I hadn't seen him in twenty years. He lived in Ohio, I was in Connecticut and the era of drop-anything-for-a-road-trip long over. I spoke to him once on the phone but the dementia had eaten away at his frontal lobe. Even Crested Butte memories got only a grunt. He handed the phone back to his wife, Kathy, and I heard him pacing in the background, asking for food as she detailed his prognosis. A month later he was gone.

The kid kept babbling. Our foggy breath rose and merged in the air before dispersing. The light over the Forest Queen–our planned lodgings– flicked off. Only the Grubstake lit the night and of course the river of stars. The kid's knees buckled with each step. *He's not shivering,* Tom said. *It's hypothermia. If we don't get him warmed up, he'll die.* Tom and Fred wrapped the kid in blankets from the trunk of our car and I jogged to the Grubstake hoping somebody knew the kid or a doctor or the local police.

The bartender said Sheriff McClung was probably home asleep. Best bet, he said, was a hospital in Gunnison 30 miles south. I started yelling,

Anybody know a kid? Late teens? Red turtleneck? Wandered off drunk? No answer. In back, four old guys in hunting gear shouted as they played poker. Empty shot glasses littered the table. *Anybody know a kid?* I asked them. *What?* A guy in an orange knit cap looked up. *Red turtleneck?* I asked. He scanned the room as if just noticing the saloon had emptied for the night.

He jumped up, yelled, *Where's my son?* and grabbed me by the collar. *We found him on the street,* I said, told him the story. He loosened his grip. *He needs a doctor,* I said. *Follow me.* The four of them grumbled and growled as I led them out into the street. The slap of frigid air shut everyone up. They sobered up. Or maybe just got madder. The kid was bundled in the Olds with the lights on, the heat blasting. Tom massaged the kid's hands to get blood flowing. Orange Cap Dad grabbed his son and yanked him from the car.

Get him to the hospital in Gunnison, Tom said. *You need to hurry.* One of the guys ran to get their car. The dad slapped the boy. *I told you not to wander off!* They laid him down in the back of their dark Ford wagon, gunned it forward and turned around. We stood in the beams of the Olds' headlights. The doors flung open, the interior washed in yellow light. Our friendship sealed by this story good enough to tell even now when I'm old enough to be the man on the porch. I knew then I'd stay with Tom and Fred in Crested Butte.

Tom wanted the listener to feel what it was like—to see us as heroes. Fred wanted a dry laugh at the cruelty. *No good deed,* he'd say. I want the story to survive us, to transfer it to your memory when we're gone.

The station wagon stopped and the dad rolled down the window, patted the rifle beside him. *If I find out you gave him drugs,* he said, *I'll come back and kill you.* We were too tired to argue. *Just hurry,* Tom said. They drove off, the right blinker flashing for no reason. We watched them until the road turned onto the highway. *Something tells me we won't see those blankets again,* Fred said. I imagined the kid propped on his elbows, watching us out the back window. And that used to be where the story ended: the three us shaking our heads.

But with Fred gone and Tom a thousand miles away in Florida and the details getting harder to recall (An orange cap? Did he really cackle?), I wonder what the boy remembers. He'd be 64 now or 65 with kids, maybe grandkids. I wonder how he tells the story of almost dying one night under the stars in Crested Butte. I can see it from his perspective: Tom, Fred and I in the headlights, growing smaller and smaller until we are nothing but memory.

Unruly Love

Unruly Sonnet

I keep trying to corral Amy and Carl into fourteen lines but they break out
alone and together.
       Amy visits us, her daughter a wounded bird in her lap, says
Sex hurts! I've got books, flowers, Lizzie. I'm done with love, leaving the details
of her drink-demolished marriage unspoken.
         Then Carl appears, sandy-haired saint,
scooping them both in his arms, luring Amy back into the open, humming softly
to Lizzie. We all clap in bewildered delight.
        And just when
I've steered them into stanzas, Amy comes north alone, slips me a photo of Carl
in a black dress wearing red lipstick and eye shadow, says,
            She's Colleen now.
It's weird to feel her boobs in my back when we spoon. Amy raises a glass.
To Carl! To Colleen! We drink.
       She posts photos of crocuses and Kerouac.
The turn comes too soon. *Amy died Christmas Eve in her sleep, Colleen writes.*
Lizzie and I are heartbroken.
      They drive north that summer with ashes. We balance
on Amy's old dock. *Say goodbye to Mommy,* Colleen whispers to Lizzie,
who's curled into her chest
       and they shovel cinder and bone in high arcs into the bay.

Hannah

Hannah was born months too soon, lungs still wet, resisting doctors' efforts
to pop them open, but she was beautiful even in her tininess. In the hour
Barb held her, she imagined Hannah's first babbling, first Mary Janes,
first wobbly bike ride, first bra, first boy, first book that changed her life,
first prom gown, first Pulitzer, first baby born.

As Hannah's body cooled,
Ray stood over the bed, kissed her soft head. *Goodbye, sweet thing*, he said.
She's not a thing, Barb said. *But she is sweet,* Ray insisted. *Don't take her far,*
Barb said to the nurse who lifted Hannah off her chest, *we're going to bury her.*
Celebrate this birth day, Barb said to herself, hold her picture in our hearts.
Some thought them odd for refusing to forget, but Hannah was alive, if only for
an hour

and kicking in the womb for months, growing in their dreams for years.
When Hannah's sister and brother were born, they dreamed their own Hannah—
sharing their secrets, holding her in their mind's eye, honoring her being.
At sixteen they shared a cake. At twenty-one they raised a beer: *To Hannah.*

Moving On

Sarah met Frank two years after losing Dick to cancer. *No marriage,* she said,
I'm not going through that again. They had seven years of dancing, cruises,
and dry martinis before he got sick. Then she moved to live with her children.

Jill left when the kids were young to start a new life with her boss.
When her cancer came, Jim took Jill back, drove her to chemo, laid out her meds,
spoon fed and bathed her, made sure, he said, she got a proper goodbye.

When Rick died, Sandi moved back from Florida and sang in the choir.
When Jean died, Ronnie played golf every day and volunteered at church.
When Nick died, Carol doubled down on grandchildren—and prayer.

Clare's grandfather lost two wives to cancer. When the third got sick,
he brought her to the garage, closed the door, and turned on the Buick.
They talked about the day they met, were found arm in arm in the morning.

A husband in his nineties grew violent from Alzheimer's until he fell in love
with a newcomer to his ward. His wife visits with flowers for his new girl.

Prepping for the Test

It's 8:30 in Fairfield, yes, August 20, a Saturday morning
and I'm studying for the Montreal Cognitive Assessment
and like a Frank O'Hara poem I start with where and when I am.
The heat wave has finally broken

        and I repeat my name aloud,
like I'm mentally checking for ten fingers and ten toes
as if just entering the world rather than delaying my departure.

The grass has browned because I forgot to turn on the sprinkler
and I repeat the five words: *Face, Velvet, Church, Red, Daffodil.*

I've avoided early death by dune buggy like O'Hara
or renegade genes like my poor neighbor, Andrew,
and still dream of a late prime in my mid-sixties. Maybe
I'd be better off exercising my brain by learning Mandarin
or doing puzzles like those nonagenarian nuns in Minnesota.
I draw a chair, then draw a line from the 1 to A to 2 to B
on the form I've copied off the internet.

        I never used to study for tests,
taking the SAT with a hangover, and even taking my driver's test
after one quick read through the book. I know better now. The real tests
—Anne's breast cancer, raising children, my mother's slow decline
—were all pop quizzes I stumbled through. I read the sentences aloud

and repeat them, say the five words again: *Face, Velvet, Church, Red,
Daisies?* and wonder if a story would help: I'm in church facing an altar
where velvet drapes hang beside the red of Jesus's wounds. The daffodils
wave in flower beds out front. Does this test have a Christian bias?
Is a dementia diagnosis one more privilege?

        My head hurts
and I think of the NFL adjusting their tests for concussion money
and depressing Black players' scores. Is dementia also caused by self-induced

collisions with booze and smokes and bad genes and too many hot dogs?
I balance on one leg as I study to reduce my risk of falling.

I name the animals: *tiger, penguin, owl.* And read the numbers,
close my eyes, repeat them aloud. When my friend Eileen was studying
to be a school psychologist, I helped her practice giving IQ tests
and messed up the numbers going forward by trying to group them
but remembered more going backwards when I just listened, repeating them
like a song: 8, 7, 3, 9, 2... Like notes. Like a bird call.
Trying to remember interfered with remembering.
                                        I draw a chair,
read a list of letters, tap each E, and begin counting backward
from a hundred by sevens: 100, 93, 86, wondering if there's a pattern
I'm missing, bringing myself back to the task: 79, 72...
Or are we all just inventing patterns? And shouldn't I want to know
if I have dementia? I repeat the words: *Face, Church, Velvet
Red, Daffodils.* Do they need to be in order? Do plurals count?
                                    Like O'Hara, I'm sweating now.
Out the window, the bird feeder looks empty. I probably shouldn't fill it
in summer. Is there a point where you just let nature do its work?

I tally the points, 30 out of 30—well past the 25 I need to pass
—feeling tired, calm like after meditating, hungry, wanting to write.
Out the window, a cardinal lands on the feeder, finds a last morsel,
sings a high *shear, shear, shear*, then *witwitwitwit* and flies away.

Curse of a Boyfriend Scorned

May you stub your toe, ding your elbow
on the doorframe, knock your knee on the computer desk,
crack the shell of a cavity on bacon gristle,
get a blistering sunburn on the first day of spring.

May your children be pigeon-toed and math-challenged,
your husband suffer from high cholesterol and torn rotator cuffs,
your mother become forgetful before her time, your sister
marry a know-it-all who talks too loud at Christmas dinner.

May you forget why you chose someone else, why he seemed
funnier, handsomer—a more promising prospect. May you stop
on a day like today when gray clouds cover the sun and ask
if life may have been perfect on a different path. Until then

may your cat have hairballs, may your basement leak, may you
wander the house wondering what it was you set out to do.

Too Young Lovers

Whenever we got past first base,
my ninth-grade girlfriend'd ask, *Do you love me?*
What is love? I'd wonder. More than the lust
I burned with on her playroom couch.

I don't know, I'd say and we'd stall again
at second base, both lying back, panting,
staring at the tiled ceiling, questioning:
What did I love? Was it all *want, want, want?*

Just tell her "Yes," my suave friend Sean insisted,
like she was just asking for a password.
Was I the good guy for refusing to lie or just
one more jerk she'd learn to cast aside and overcome?

Fifty years later, on this December Sunday, I google and find
her standing next to the tall, goateed guy who said *Yes.*

Rolling Home

They flew from Ireland for my brother's wedding. Hugh packed his wool pants, three pairs of long underwear, three bottles of Jameson's. Teresa, Granny's sister, was wee beside him, red-cheeked, gray-haired. We had to lean in to decipher her bubbling brogue. Married late, they shared a kind of winking love that came after they'd learned to live without. Hugh, 70, fit from rowing out to his lobster pots, sang a trembling tenor we'd beg for. *I need a little of the birdseed first,* he'd say. We'd rush out to make hot toddies with Jameson's, hot water, sugar and lemon, and sway as he sang, *Rolling home, rolling home, rolling home across the sea.*

By the time we visited Ireland, Hugh had passed. His lobster boat sat on blocks in the yard. Aunt Teresa still bubbled, pausing only at the mention of his name. She drove us to all the ruins, crossing herself furiously at the passing graveyards. At night when we thanked her, said, *See you tomorrow,* she'd say, *God willin'.*

Eight years later she joined him. *Rolling home to dear old Ireland.* Sometimes love leaves an imprint time can't wash away. *Rolling home so fair to thee.*

To A Flirt

After Horace, I.v

Who's wrapped around your frail finger now?
Who's fallen into those cold blues?

Who thinks that love has found a home
in the echo of your laugh? What empty-

headed dolt is teaching you to dance?
How he will replay these scenes,

lamenting his missteps, misspeaks,
missed opportunities, never suspecting

he's just another in a long line of lost links
in the endless chain now missing you.

As for me, I untether myself from you
with no illusion that I'll be remembered.

One less fool infatuated with your pale clavicles,
devilish touch, that sweet *uhsh* you made in love.

The Picture that Came with the Frame

could be his wife caught glancing
over a narrow shoulder—a look of come-here
or I'll-be-there, both steadfast and saucy,
a desktop reminder to stop for eggs, to hurry home.

Two children framed in the same 5x7 silver—
a girl, tan-armed in Easter dress; a paler boy
in corduroy. They favor their mother. Their steady smiles
make late-night work both worth the pain and lonesome.

The corner space they occupy amid the office clutter
stakes a claim to a life beyond gray cubby screens–a ticket
to water cooler chitchat: *He's a pistol, that boy.*
I'm a lucky man, for sure. But it's not enough.

If he could catch the pose and light, slip into a store-shelf frame,
angle the frames tight, they'd kiss good morning, kiss goodnight.

Christmas Pictures

It's bad luck to send such handsome photos
of the children. Don't draw attention
to good fortune; the Fates wait with plastic
hammers to smash the heads of fools
who smile too brightly, shout too gleefully.
Pass on all chain letters. Knock on wood.
Let someone else volunteer to fly the flag of reason;
it's not you they'll drown, but those you love.

But the call to crow is so alluring:
the chorus of Mi, mi, mi, my, my, mine,
my gifted scribe, scholar, soccer striker,
the fragile face of youth and promise.

No. Stifle pride. Keep their heads low. Understate.
Compliment your neighbor. Buy another year of joy.

Don't Love Anything Too Much

Loving works both ways—like metaphor.
Cords attach at both ends, two unlike things
get wrapped and wrapped until one becomes
the other—ground in the same gravity.

So don't let anything love you too much.
Don't let anyone grab you by the ankles,
massage your sore neck, whisper in your ear.
Cut the ropes that anchor, lift the lines looped
around that rotting pier. Don't let anyone
throw sandbags in your basket, keep you moored,
unable to rise through clouds, through ether,
soar in the sweet silence of your own space.

And don't love any one or thing too much.
Quitting's harder than dodging love's first touch.

Spring Wedding

The two ailing rhododendrons look like great aunts dressed for a wedding,
the last they'll attend: bright red lipstick on pale powdered faces,
too large flowers pinned to their frail chests.
                                        I was ready to dig them up
before the buds began to open for the first time in three years, since an icy winter
hit them like a stroke: withering roots, snapping branches, sapping leaves
of their oily green sheen. I'd already pulled out the third sister after she shriveled
down to two brown leaves. I'd ordered three new shrubs.

But then a seam appeared on the taller bush. Other buds soon opened
like rockets ready to launch. One by one, blossoms burst in a mind-clearing red.
I put away my shovel, hid the replacement rhodies, and the ladies
made the spring wedding after all, taking their place in the receiving line
with the boxwoods and azaleas that hide the cables, pipes and meters
that line our foundation,
                        one space left empty for the sister who went first,
their limbs thin, pallor dusty, barely standing, but gloriously red in farewell.

Getting Rid of the Body

I.

I don't spend much time visiting parents' graves.
What's gone is gone and I've got nothing to say
to the dead. I'd smiled when my mother said
Dad would love this view, pointing to the meadow
below his plot. She was imagining her view, I bet,
lying beside him as if holding hands.
That's one reason old people return to religion
in the end—for a view better than the soil
and being eaten by worms muscling you through
the cave of their ribbed intestines and out their other ends
into the relative dark of loosened earth
—sun only accidently seeping through.

II.

A cemetery in town is bordered on one side
by the Mill River and the other by an algae pond
and ringed by trees tall enough to block out the lights
and give a clear view of summer constellations
and hilly enough for a bike ride past headstones
and obelisks and crosses and Virgin Marys
and mausoleums. The only ones I know there
are a student, Justin, dead from an overdose,
now beneath a small flat marker;
and Mary Tyler Moore, whose shrine is fenced in.
Her casket-length stone reads *After All* at the top.
These markers are for the survivors to visit
but what of the survivors' survivors and theirs?
The memories decompose faster than the wood and stone.

III.

One of the first things to go is your brain.

Without oxygen, cells self-destruct,
spilling all that fluid onto the coffin floor.
Hungry microbes that normally help digest
escape, reach your liver and gallbladder,
bile floods the body, staining it yellow-green.
Toxic gases expand and cause your body to bloat,
stink. Your blood vessels deteriorate, iron spills out,
becoming brownish-black. Tissues collapse
into watery mush. Cotton clothes disintegrate.
The fat in your butt turns to soap-like grave wax.
Bones crack leaving brittle mineral frame behind..
The last collapses into dust. Only teeth remain.
Teeth, grave wax, and nylon threads.

IV.

At Grandpa's wake, my first, he was well preserved:
pink and still and rubbery, lying in a red satin-lined casket.
I hadn't seen him since he walked into a snowy night
in his boxer shorts. Hardening of the arteries, they said.
My second funeral was Nanny's. I remember the wake,
her ex-boyfriend Zeke smoking through the hole
in his throat and talking with a vibrating machine,
and the undertakers playing cards in a back room
on a green felt table waiting for the mourners to leave.
At Aunt Rose's wake, the cousins in front of me
spoke aloud their goodbyes as they knelt
by the open casket, then stood and kissed her farewell.
My mother's wake was like a reunion—all stories
and laughter. Zak said, *What a great party!*

V.

There's three things we can do with your mum,
the undertaker says in *Monty Python's Flying Circus.*
We can bury her, burn her, or dump her ...

If we burn her, she gets stuffed in the flames,
crackle, crackle, crackle, which is a bit of a shock
if she's not quite dead, but quick ... and then we give you
a handful of ashes, which you can pretend are hers ...
If we bury her, she gets eaten up—lots of weevils,
and nasty maggots ... which as I said before
is a bit of a shock if she's not quite dead.
Or eat her ... roasted with a few French fries,
broccoli, horseradish sauce ... some parsnips.
If you feel a bit guilty about it after,
we can dig a grave and you can throw up in it.

VI.

Back at Mom's grave, I have to admit
the view is excellent, though
more headstones now clutter the meadow.
There's just not room for us all.
I know some city cemeteries
are the only place for a family picnic
on the grass or a night time rendezvous
for teenagers to kiss and drink beer,
but why not make it a park? Just grass and trees
with the occasional sculptural nod to God
or history? Or can only the dead save us
from our urge to build, build, build?
Can't we honor and remember without
rows and rows of dates on granite?

VII.

I haven't earned a sky burial by Tibetan monks,
my chopped-up body fed to birds who can fly
my soul to heaven; or a pyre launched on the Ganges
by Hindu priests sending my body off to the next life;
or having my remains eaten by Wari people of Brazil

in order to expel the fear and mystery; or a launch
in a death ship by Vikings, who also liked a good burn,
to bring my body back to the gods.
The Haida crushed their chiefs to pulp with clubs
and sealed them in totems outside their homes.
South Koreans bake the ashes to a shine, make a shrine
of death beads in a bowl to keep the soul from wandering.
I am due nothing from faith or achievement
and must invent my own quiet goodbye.

VIII.

Burning and spreading is the way I'll go
from a death drone flying some winter day
off a beach in Bermuda or Laguna
spreading ashes over waves as it circles with the birds.
Or over the cemetery with Mary T. and Justin
but no flowers to plant and water,
no grand pretense of lasting significance.
There is indeed comfort in imagining the view.
Can I state my wishes in a poem?
Can I burn my ashes to such fine dust
no child ever thinks she's found beach treasure,
brings it to her mother and asks, *What's this?*
And no mother has to crinkle her nose
and say, *Nothing, honey. Just throw it away.*

FOUND POEM SOURCE for Section III: "What Happens to the Human Body After 100 Years Inside a Coffin?" Gina Echevarria and Shira Polan, *Business Insider*, August 16, 2019.

FOUND POEM SOURCE for Section V: *Monty Python's Flying Circus: Just the Words.* Chapman, Graham, et al, edited by Roger Wilmut, London: Methuen, 1989.

Noble Suffering

Leaving a Light On

In some ways suffering ceases to be suffering at the moment it finds a meaning.
                                        —*Viktor Frankl*

A friend sends a quote he keeps above his desk. He says it's from the Buddha.
A person needs three things to be truly happy: someone to love, something to do,
and something to hope for. On the bottom of the email, he writes, *Pretty true!*

When I feed the quote into Google, Tom Bodett pops up as the author—
the Motel Six guy, who says, *We'll leave a light on for you* and I start a theory
that love is not enough—that hope is a light we all need to keep blazing.

But Elvis and Kant are also listed as sources—all jostling for space on my wall
of inspirations. I trace the quote to a clergyman, George Washington Burnap.
No Buddha, but still *Pretty true!* And curiously close to Victor Frankl,

whose search for meaning found three paths: *find someone to love, find*
something to do, or suffer nobly (as we hope our suffering serves a purpose).
Except Burnap, Bodett and the Buddha demand all three for happiness.

I pin both quotes like to-do lists above my desk: keep cultivating love,
find something to do, hope for happiness—knowing I'll get my chance to suffer.

Two Blossoms

The young woman knew she would die in the next few days.
But when I talked to her she was cheerful in spite
of this knowledge.
                              I am grateful that fate has hit me so hard,
she told me. *In my former life I was spoiled*
and did not take spiritual accomplishments seriously.

Pointing through the window of the hut, she said,
This tree here is the only friend I have in my loneliness.

Through that window, she could see just one branch
of a chestnut tree, and on that branch were two blossoms.

I often talk to this tree, she said to me. I was startled
and didn't quite know how to take her words. Was she delirious?
Did she have occasional hallucinations?
                              Anxiously I asked her
if the tree replied. *Yes.* What did it say to her? She answered,
It said to me, 'I am here—I am here—I am life, eternal life.'

FOUND POEM SOURCE: *Man's Search for Meaning: An Introduction to Logotherapy.*
Viktor E. Frankl. Translated by Ilse Lasch, Beacon Press, 2006.

It Takes a Minute After Gil Wakes to Remember She's Gone

He looks at Cindy's side of the bed, at the empty space, remembers her snoring
and how she denied it. *I think I'd know if I was snoring.* In a flash of memory
he hears her say, *Time to change the sheets.*

                        Cindy'd smiled when he visited,
even after she couldn't remember him and called him Jason, thinking
he was her brother. She'd tuck her legs under her like a schoolgirl
and grin at the pictures of her roses, or ones he took of the kitchen
or bed so she'd know he was keeping things clean.

Imagine if I had died first? he says aloud, *She'd be lost!* With a groan,
he rolls out of bed, takes a shower, eats breakfast, grabs her pruning shears
and gloves, and goes out to the roses. *Don't overwater!* he can hear her say
as he kneels in the dirt. *They're beautiful!* Gil looks up at his old neighbor,
a white dog leashed at his side. Gil was afraid he'd said that aloud himself.
They're Cindy's.

                      He snips one, puts it in a vase on the table, eats lunch,
cleans the dishes and floors, takes a Polaroid, slips it in his pocket.

Not Her

She decided to tell the children after Thanksgiving dinner
but was afraid she'd forget—afraid that early onset wasn't early enough
so she wrote each a note to say how she loved them. When the day arrived

she remembered and, once they'd scraped the pie plates clean, she told them
and Jenny cried and Dylan patted her arm and Lee Ann yelled that doctors
don't know everything. And Peter googled a list of specialists and homes.

And the grandchildren asked what Gommy meant, and the spouses calmed them
in the other room. When their father'd faded to a bitter child, the kids checked in
but left the care to her for five long years. He'd always seemed old. Not her.

Now they stumbled through the dawning of their grief. She soothed each in turn.
Lee Ann moved beside her. Dylan began to cry. Jenny took the list. Peter shouted
and paced. Finally they quieted. She hugged them tight and sent them home.

She didn't tell them about their father's fentanyl, stashed bit by bit,
or her plan to sink beneath her bath water and save them from it all.

Old Couples

Anne asks me to stop sending her pictures of cute old couples when I travel.
It's depressing! she texts after my *That's us someday!* under eighty-somethings
in Iowa City, walking ahead of me into town under an August blue sky.
They'd finally found the same easy pace: she with her walker, he with his cane.

My mother groans at the silver-haired couples at her assisted living,
reminded of the ache in her hip where dad, even more in dementia,
had been firmly attached—now only in dreams. Sometimes I watch her sleep,
her eyes fluttering beneath pale lids, her fingers curling as if holding a hand.

Bob pedals next to me at the town gym: tall, ramrod straight. The caretaker's
off today so his wife sits in a chair by the door, hemmed in by her walker.
She thinks she's just returned from her mother's wedding in Toledo.
Long trip, I say. She frowns, nods at Bob. *Ask him if he's done.*

She was nineteen when I married her, Bob says when I say it's got to be tough.
He shrugs. *It is what it is what it is,* he says. *We had 62 good years.*

On the Drive to Uncle Pete's

Beside me in the old V Dub, Granny waited
as if dormant, as if cars had just been invented,
as if practicing her Irish training to be still until the hated
Black and Tans had passed, as if that war had never ended.

At sixteen, her silence mystified me. Her joyless ride
day after day terrified me. To get a rise, I tried
asking if her priest-son Pete had nun honeys on the side.
I'd said I'd joined the priesthood, then admitted I had lied.

Except for one *Oh Jackie!* she waited, silent as a stone
–like looking out the window at the lawn when we were home,
nodding off to sleep, jolting straight awake—always alone.
For what? I'd often wonder. She kept her thoughts her own.

So I sped up, beeped the horn, wildly gesticulated.
She stared still straight ahead and waited, and waited.

Waiting

Oh, Jackie, there were no cars when I was young in Clenchagora.
A horse if you were lucky. Or rich. The family I went to live with at 12
had a horse for the farm and a horse for the carriage, but I was inside
tending the baby. Even New York had more horses than cars when I arrived.

Oh, Jackie, when your grandpa moved us to Suffield, he said, *It looks like Ireland,*
but the fields had too many trees and the wrong green and cows instead of sheep.
But I went. Left sisters and brothers in the Bronx. And all your mother's cousins.
When the husband says go, you go, but I didn't have to be happy.

Oh, Jackie, I know I said a man up to my knee is worth a dozen women,
but I didn't like it. It was the way. I survived. And when your grandpa died
and your dad moved me down with you, what could I do? Help cook and clean.
Again a mother's helper. Oh, Jackie, when it's my time, I am ready.

But the man upstairs decides. Sometimes when I look out my window
the grass is a Clenchagora green. If I close my eyes, I can smell it.

Last Chance

Before he died, I told my father everything I did as a kid,
a friend of friend told me. *All the drugs and lies,*
the sneaking out, the booze I stole, the school I skipped.
Just in time, he said. *Dad died a month later.*

You ever think that's what killed him? I asked. I mean,
his dad made it to old age, his kids were still visiting, he figured
he'd done one thing right. Why make him feel stupid?

I overslept for my college graduation and raced to the fieldhouse
picturing my parents trying to pick me out of a robed crowd
of six thousand. The ceremony ended as I arrived, but I found a friend
and pumped him for info: Best speaker? Worst? Highlights? Screw ups?

I went to lunch with my parents, shook my head with my dad
about the boring valedictorian, nodded at the brilliance of the featured speaker.
What was the chancellor wearing? I asked. *Where were you anyways?*

They'd driven five hours so I laughed when they talked about trying
to find me in a sea of black when my school stood en masse,
told them they guessed right—I was five robes to the left of the blonde
with the plastic chicken on her mortarboard. And they drove home happy.

Now I'm sixty-seven and forgetting something new every day
or learning something new I should have known all along.
When my kids start to tell me about the notes they forged

or the girls they snuck into their bedrooms, I want to give them a hug
and beg them to let me live with my illusions. But I know confession
is for the sinners not the sinned. So I imagine that other old dad
and do what he did: sit on my hands, face them square and listen.

Winter Birds

I keep thinking they missed their cue
seduced by some false November sun
and now suffering for their sins.
Such scrawny legs and feet, translucent claws!

Yet they survive: chickadee, junco
nuthatch, cardinal searching for seeds,
spiders, tree buds, fluffing their feathers
for warmth—alone, in pairs or flocks
that litter my yard or string themselves
in black rosaries across the sky.

In a blizzard they disappear, huddling,
I hope, in hedges, the downwind side of trees.
In the morning sun, a nuthatch flutters in a backyard fir,
tooting his horn like an answered prayer.

State of the Union

Now that they're alone, Phil's chewing sounds louder. *And do you need*
to scrape the plate for every last scrap? Clare asks. *At least,* he says,
I don't put my shoes on the bed. Or say "et cetera" when I mean "et al."

Our neighbor Eve tells us about her husband's *man cold,* his dramatic sniffles.
Even when he takes her to the hospital to pass her kidney stone,
he begs the nurse for a lozenge. *Men!* I join in since I'm outnumbered.

You must put the tines down for safety, June says, putting forks in the dishwasher.
Oscar shakes his head for the thousandth time. *Tines down, they never get clean.*

Our friends argue in the car. She shouts, *Did you see that truck? Are you blind?*
He swears, smacks the wheel. *Shut up!* We wonder: *Can this marriage be saved?*
He parks, they smile, he helps with her coat. She asks if she can carry his camera.

Now that I'm retired my wife has more time to stare at me. *You yawn a lot.*
she says. *Your nostrils are too small.* With the children up and gone, I distract her
with the dog, the TV, ask about her day. These nostrils aren't getting any bigger.

Surrender

Love Again

Fifty years later, on this December Sunday, I google and find her
standing next to the tall, goateed guy who said *Yes*.
                                                    The next image
shows her book about what to do when this man you'd waited decades for
writes you a note, balances the accounts on the desktop, leaves, comes back
to open an old Valentine's card on the screen, hoping it's the first thing
you'll find when you learn he is gone, drives off, and parks close enough
to the veteran's hospital for his organs to be shared—

                                                    and how to crawl,
then kneel, then struggle upright, to use psychics and poets, the Buddha
and blessings, gurus and God and the grass beneath your bare feet, and
writing the book to step back into the light—about how to grieve, yes,
but also how to love yourself enough to come through it, how to push
and how to fall backward,
                              trusting the world to catch you.
In the opposite arc of her first love story, she moves from sun into darkness,
making it back most days to partly cloudy, ready to be loved again.

Tying Granny to a chair was wrong, of course

but she had been warned. When she gripped the table,
pulled herself up and said, *Napkins!* I said, *I'll get 'em.*

I didn't say, *You'll fall and we'll be sopping up your blood
with paper towels.* And when she pushed herself up for the salt,
I said, *I got it. Relax! Let. Us. Eat.*

Whenever my parents went out, Granny'd try to take charge.
Even Ellen was saying, *Stop it, Granny.* But Granny
just laughed. When she got up for the butter, I said,

If you get up again, I'm tying you to the chair. I was joking,
but she took it as a challenge, so when Ellen asked for the ketchup

and Granny pushed herself up, I said, *That's it!* went to the pantry,
got some rope, looped it around her waist and tied it to the chair.

And it worked. In fact, we forgot about it until we finished dessert
and cleared the table. I was at the sink rinsing plates, when I heard,
Jackie? TUNK! Jackie? TUNK! and turned to see her struggling to her feet,

then falling back from the weight of the chair. *Jackie? TUNK!*
Her face red from laughing—making a big show of it. *Jackie? TUNK!*
Pulling the knots tighter and tighter. Took ten minutes to get them loose.

So now forty years later when I dream we've had another baby,
she looks like my son Zak, but black haired with Granny's blue eyes.

I'm rocking her to sleep in the chair in Zak's nursery with his name
painted in red and blue on the top rail. She begins a soft baby snore
and settles into my chest like I'm a hammock.

The chair parts squeak in a steady rhythm and I'm afraid to stop.
Out the window, it's pouring—an August heat-clearing rain.

Large drops ricochet off the street white against the black tar.
I wake in my dark bedroom to *TUNK! TUNK!*
I wait for a *Jackie!* Or the sound of Granny laughing.

No Place That Does Not See You

After Rainier Maria Rilke

My wife's California cousins are avid huggers, so I kept a body between us,
used Tai Kwon Do to block their attacks, avoid their grips, their breasts smashed
into my chest, my arms useless, pinned to my side.

For we Irish, hugs—like tears
and I-love-yous—are reserved for drunks and aunts at wakes. Then my son
was born with Anne's big eyes and the hugging gene. I struggled to adapt.
But when Will taught my mother to hug, I thought, why not me?

Hugging, I realized, was committing, and I preferred sitting on the sidelines
and making fun of the players. So I studied Will's techniques:
his hug initiation, duration, variation, withdrawal. I read articles like
"11 Benefits of Hugging—Backed by Chemistry."

Like Temple Grandin
taking visitors to a Pacific sunset, I tried not to check my watch until it was over.
Now I start the cousin hugs. Sure I still miss cues, have to make u-turns
on the stairs and give my wife the hug she needs.

But when I hug friends and
feel their arms dangling, I tell them what I learned: You must embrace your life.

An Old Woman Sits in a Lawn Chair in Her Driveway

A white dog in her lap. *Where did you come from?* she asks and scratches him be-hind the ear. She knows it's a sunny day, the big maple gives her shade, and she should stand up and begin the long walk home. Her husband steps out of their garage, hands her a sandwich, stretches his back with a groan and sits beside her. *Did I miss anything?* he asks. She turns to him and smiles. *What?* He laughs, faces the street before them and waves to the man walking a dog, the mother riding bikes with her two small children, the pregnant blonde pushing a stroller. He looks down the street to the avenue where cars drive by too fast, imagines their blinkers winking before turning onto the ramp, merging onto the interstate, accelerating to slip between rumbling semis, past signs welcoming them to state after state, crossing rivers, skirting lakes. Above, silver planes circle the blue planet orbiting its fiery sun afloat in a milky spiral in our dark universe. *Quite a day?* he says. She looks at him, says, *What?* With a sweep of his hand, he says, *The day.* She takes a bite, says, *Hmm.*

Confession

Bless me father for I have sinned, I began,
hoping as always the priest didn't recognize my voice
and hoping this time he didn't recognize my sins.
It has been four weeks since my last confession.

While waiting in the pews, my brother and I had concocted a plan
to figure out the worth in prayers for every sin.
I pictured a list tacked inside the priest's compartment
(One lie = one Hail Mary, Disobeyed mother = two Our Fathers).

I lied to my father two times, I said, making sure I got it right,
and lied to my mother once. It had to match his sins exactly
as we planned it out in whispers, hands covering our mouths
so our words didn't echo off the vaulted St. Catherine's ceiling
and attract the attention of the nuns pacing in black and white.
I fought with my brother three times I whispered, *and my sister twice.*

Donny had gone first, putting the same sins
in a different order and adding one extra at the end.
That would be the key. The priest, Father Naughton, I think,
seemed to have a cold, judging by his wheezing.

Or maybe he was just old and I was now paying more attention.
I wonder why religion never stuck. Our uncle was a priest,
our parents devout, our grandparents almost pagan Irish Catholic
and here we were—me in fifth grade, Donny in eighth

—trying to game the confession system. *I was mean to a friend.*
Naughton's shadowed head leaned into the grate between us.
I yelled at Granny. We could have certainly used a little religion
to set us straight. Instead, I stole Nanny's cigarettes
and Donny filched my father's booze. We learned from experience
the cost of lying, of stealing, of shouting things we couldn't take back.

Donny was better at pretending, but even fifty years later,
we're still suspicious of pat answers, still rankle when told what to do.
When I paused, Father Naughton said, *And?* and waited.
Oh, right, I said. *I am sorry for these and all my sins.*

But I wasn't. It was all an act with lines we'd both memorized,
except Naughton imagined an audience of one, high above us,
perhaps stroking his grey beard, and I just had Donny waiting at the altar.
I carefully memorized my penance to compare it to his.

It's strange how I still reject it all, but wish I could believe.
Imagine a world where every regret can be wiped clean,
every doubt washed to clarity, every question answered.
When I walked up the aisle to say my penance, saw Donny ahead,
kneeling and pretending to pray, Jesus above him in all his tortured beauty,
I thought we'd learn the system, soon have our own list of the costs of sin.

Love Poems

Anne says, *Stop writing depressing poems!* when I share one about a grandmother
with early dementia planning to sink into her bath water. *It's a love poem,* I say.
She's saving her children from suffering. But Anne shakes her head. *She's dying.*

Sandra says, *I'm just glad to see him happy again,* when her husband
with dementia falls in love. It's sad and beautiful to love someone that much.
It takes skill and will to adapt to the cruel facts of this world.
                                                    When Amy died,
Colleen scooped Lizzie up in cupped hands and said, *We will get through this.*
Gil climbed out of bed to tend Cindy's roses. Sharon is ready for new love.

I tell Anne a joke: After her husband died, Betty, 90, said, *Best time to do it*
at our age is when the church bells ring. Nice and slow and even. In
on the Ding and out on the Dong.
                                    Betty paused to wipe a tear. *He'd still be alive*
if that ice cream truck hadn't come along. Anne smiles at me but doesn't laugh.

There's an old couple with a cane and a walker in Iowa City still headed to town.
I want us to meet them for lunch, share their banter, study her wink, his shy grin.

Tough Love

As you can see I'm dying, the professor said to open our first class. His face,
worn to gray skin and bone, left no doubt. Ridged brows shadowed his dark eyes.
For fourteen weeks, you will learn about group therapy by doing, he said.

He stared down questions. The stillness demanded secrets. After thirty minutes
a shaggy-haired guy said, *I'm having an affair with a patient.* The professor
nodded and the details spilled out. The next week an hour in, an ex-nun confessed

she'd aborted her child. *Oh, you must have*—I began but his glare shut me down.
She told us everything. Each week we sat in silence until someone cracked.
I'd interrupt, offer them a chance to reconsider, he'd scowl. One night, he waited,

a grim shadow in the fluorescent hall, and said, *Stop trying to save everyone.*
I nodded. *They need to speak.* After we got into our dark cars, he lit a cigarette.
The orange flared on his skeletal face. The next week we learned he was dead.

Our talk echoed strangely in the room. *We want to finish class like he taught us,*
we said and then sat in the hammer of silence until someone split open.

Surrender

The river was higher than when we'd forded in the fall, but it was late
and this wide bend in the Housatonic was still the shallowest spot.

So we re-cinched our tents and bags, strapped on our packs and,
under a cloud-shrouded moon, began crossing—Guy first, then Tom
and Sarah, me at the rear for clean-up.

                    At sixteen, camping had become
the only time I wasn't fighting to make my life my own. Guy crossed
like a summer stroller, but the lovebirds wobbled. *Keep your head down,*

I shouted above the river's roar. *Test each step.* They screamed at the current.
Be the river, I yelled. They laughed, slowed, clasped hands, alternated steps.
I walked in a low stance, spotting with arms held wide.

                    Sarah then Tom
climbed up the opposite bank with a *Whoop!* and a *Yes!* I relaxed and looked up
as the moon broke free of the clouds and laid a rippling sword of reflection

right down the river into my gut. With an *Oof,* I fell back, floating, surrendering
to the current, a contented speck of the quick river, white moon, black night.

End Notes

"How to Hold a Heart" is a found poem from "Tip: How to Hold a Heart," Malia Wollan, *New York Times*, Jan. 8, 2016. Malia Wollan's writing in the *Tip* column of the Sunday *New York Times Magazine* frequently approached poetry and, in this case, makes a perfect half sonnet.

"On Turning 61" is for Katie Moyse, who must be at least 62 by now.

"Every Snowflake" Most sources credit the Greeks with naming seven kinds of love. Some say four or six, but a few also mention mania as an eighth. In *The Four Loves,* C. S. Lewis writes about *Storge, Philia, Eros* and *Agape.* A good summary of the seven can be found in Neel Burton's "These Are the 7 Types of Love," in *Psychology Today*, January 8, 2016.

"Rejoice in the Cat" refers to an excerpt from Christopher Smart's "Jubilate Agno" about his cat Jeoffrey. Andrew Lloyd Webber's musical *Cats* is apparently based on T. S. Eliot's poetry collection, *Old Possum's Book of Practical Cats* from Faber and Faber Ltd. London, 1939.

"Old and New" Shakespeare's Sonnet LXXVI begins: "Why is my verse so barren of new pride," and ends with the lines I quote.

"Unflinching" is an *ekphrsais* inspired by Alice Neel's final self-portrait. The quotes in italics in the epigraph and in the first and last stanzas are from Alice herself; those in the middle couplet are from her daughter-in-law, Ginny Neel. Alice Neel was an inspiration for many young woman painters (including my good friend

Jude Magin Kallok) as well as many figurative painters of all genders (including my-self). The quotes come from the documentary *Alice Neel* directed by her grandson Andrew Neel, and from two articles. No author is listed for the first, "Portraits, People and Poets, The Visual Artist Alice Neel Uptown In Harlem, 1990—1984," in *Harlem World Magazine*, July 23, 2021. Tim Adams wrote, "The people of Harlem, as Painted by Alice Neel— In Pictures" published in *The Guardian*, April 29, 2017.

"Found" is a found poem from "She Is 96 and Does Not Fear Her Death. But Do Her Children?" by John Leland, *New York Times*, January 3, 2020.

"Prepping for the Test" I'd been trying and failing to write a poem about studying for the Montreal Cognitive Assessment since I brought my mother to take the test in 2012. I found a way in when I re-read Frank O'Hara's *Lunch Poems* and realized he begins many poems with the date and location, as if he were prepping for the MoCA himself.

"To a Flirt" was inspired by Horace, particularly Poem 5 in Book I of *The Odes and Carmen Saeculare of Horace*, translated by John Conington (London, George Bell and Sons, 1882).

"Getting Rid of the Body" contains two found stanzas. Stanza Three is se-lected phrases from "What happens to the Body After 100 Years Inside a Coffin?" by Gina Echevarria and Shira Polan in *Business Insider*, August 16, 2019. Stanza Five comes word for word from *Monty Python's Flying Circus* "Episode 26, The Under-taker," transcribed in *Monty Python's Flying Circus: Just the Words*, edited by Roger Wilmut (London: Methuen, 1989). The burial rituals of other cultures come from various sources including Kate Torgovnick May's "Death Is Not the End: Fascinat-ing Funeral Traditions from Around the Globe," in *Ideas.ted.com*, 1 Oct. 2013.

"Leaving a Light On" The epigraph is from Viktor E. Frankl's *Man's Search for Meaning: An Introduction to Logotherapy*, translated by Ilse Lasch (Beacon Press, 2006). My conjecture about hope and noble suffering oversimplifies Frankl's work. In a series of lectures published in 1848, Burnap, a Unitarian minister, said, "The grand essentials of happiness in this life are: something to do, something to love, and something to hope for." I think it's great advice, but given the title of his talk,

"The Sphere and Duties of Woman: A Course of Lectures," I also wish it was from the Buddha–or even Tom Bodett.

"Two Blossoms" is a found poem from Frankl's *Man's Search for Meaning: An Introduction to Logotherapy*, translated by Ilse Lasch (Beacon Press, 2006). In the text, Frankl introduces this description of his concentration camp encounter with a young woman as being "like a poem." Frankl presents the story in his discussion of noble suffering and how people can find meaning in even the most miserable circumstances. I encourage you to read or re-read the full text.

"No Place That Does Not See You" I first heard Rilke's "Archaic Torso of Apollo" recited in unison, as if a prayer for two voices, by two classmates at Sarah Lawrence College. It still sounds like a prayer to me. The classmates recited their own composite translation, taking their favorite lines and phrasings from a number of previous translations. The title and the final line I refer to are from Stephen Mitchell's translation, *Ahead of All Parting: The Selected Poetry and Prose of Rainer Maria Rilke* (Modern Library, 1995).

Acknowledgements

I need to thank the Hudson Valley Writers Center's Jennifer Franklin and the members of her "Year of the Book" poetry class where a first draft of this book was written. And thanks also to my CWP writing group (Del, Bill, Janice, Nicole, Darcy, Bob and Julie) and my Norwalk writing group (Laurel, Van, Carol and Cathy) for their close reads and great suggestions. Thanks to Amy Holman, reader and publisher-finder extraordinaire, and to my editors Betsy and Neal Delmonico for taking me back for book two. I forgot to thank Travis Denton for his help with my last collection and thanks to the many other poets and teachers who have inspired me—Joan Larkin and Terrence Hayes deserve a special mention for this book. Thanks to all the friends, neighbors and strangers who have inspired scenes and characters in the poems. When possible, permissions have been granted, or names and identifying details have been changed.

And lastly, I need to thank my family, especially my wife Anne for her support and understanding. And my children, Will, Erin and Zak, for great feedback and for being interesting, bright, funny and forgiving. And my parents, Don and Cathy, for continuing to provide material long after they're gone. And Nanny and Granny who taught me to love old people and fear their demise. I may have embellished here and there to meet the needs of the poem. I've always feared dying alone like those drunken Irish playwrights who alienated their relatives by mining every encounter for material. I am fortunate to have a family who has not yet shown me the door.

Thanks to the following journals for publishing the poems below, some in slightly different forms:

- "Last Act," "On Turning 61" and "State of the Union" in *Clementine Unbound*
- "Losing Things" and "On the Drive to Uncle Pete's" in *One Art*
- "How to Hold a Heart," "Every Snowflake," "Flirts," "Mgothger and Dgaughtger," "Nod to the Master," "Unearthed" and "To a Flirt" in *Bloom*
- "Keeper" in *San Pedro River Review*
- "Still Love" in *Coastal Shelf*
- "A Little Red" and "Rejoice in the Cat" in *Nine Muses Poetry*
- "Holding On," "Grip and Glide," "Winter Birds" and "Surrender" in *Red Eft Review*
- "Lover/Loved" in *The Leaflet* and *Verse Virtual*
- "Lover/Loved?" in *New Croton Review*
- "Bert and Kaye," "Unflinching," "Rolling Home" and "Not Her" in *Eunoia Review*
- "Provincetown, 2010" in *Passager*
- "Unruly Sonnet" in *Nixes Mate Review*
- "Curse of Boyfriend Scorned" in *Fourteen*
- "The Picture that Came with the Frame" and "Christmas Pictures" in *The Cortland Review*
- "Old Couples" in *The Westchester Review*
- "Tying Granny to a Chair was Wrong, of Course" in *Naugatuck River Review*
- "Tough Love" in *Salamander.*

Praise for *Everybody's Vaguely Familiar*:

I love Jack Powers' light touch and deep vision. *Everybody's Vaguely Familiar* is brilliant, humanistic, quick-witted and fast-paced — but the cameos of family, high school, pop icons and suburbia open seamlessly onto the sacred ground of tragedy: mortality, suffering, how we create ourselves out of nothing and are undone. In "Smokin' a Real Cool Brank," Powers' zinging lines arrive at an epiphany — "an acute awareness of my good fortune" — but that's not where the poem ends: it ends in the human predicament: illusion, desire, cussedness, our need to flirt with disaster. *Everybody's Vaguely Familiar* is a book that will last.

— D. Nurkse

The poems in Jack Powers' debut collection ... are as human as it gets, maneuvering through the emotional landscape of life with wit, a no-nonsense clarity and a touch of sarcasm. These poems are immediate, as if each one is talking specifically to you, ... offering a past, present and most importantly a future. Read this collection and celebrate what it means to be alive.

— Kevin Pilkington

Everybody's Vaguely Familiar is a funny and poignant ride through the vivid details of our everyday lives. From adolescent smoking to philtrum guards to a miscarriage, Powers captures a male voice in search of what it all adds up to—if anything. In this carefully observant collection, he appears to suggest that even though we fail the ones we love and death claims us all, the struggle is worth it, especially when family shares it with us: "I will ... /remember a beach in Rhodes// where stars littered the sky/ like luminescent river stones/ so close// we could pluck them/ from the heavens,/ offer them to each other...."

— Laurel Peterson

Jack Powers is atuned to twists of life and language — insults refitted as endearments, families defined by their troubles, great care taken with modes of recklessness, and in his deftly funny title poem ... remembering people while forgetting faces. At the start of his debut collection, he's praising the massive coronary, favoring it over the dwindling disease and dementia that took his elders. But as mortality hovers, he teases, testing wits and pulling out the good stories of lucky close calls, game grandmothers, swearing babies, and ... pretty soon, he's against the quick demise—"and the sky seemed full/ of answers."

— Amy Holman

Jack Powers' powerful debut collection grapples with existential questions of death, illness, and love. Yet it is one of the most life-affirming collections I have read. Powers' precision of language, his enormous empathy, and his razor-sharp sense of humor allow him to walk the treacherous tightrope of sentiment without ever falling into the abyss of sentimentality. He makes the reader care passionately about the quotidian troubles of his characters. Powers' command of language and his unique voice offer a profound and affecting glimpse of dashed dreams; boyhood exploits; a miscarriage; dementia; deaths of parents, students, friends; and a unique brush with death at age twenty-nine. The persona is as nuanced as the character in a novel. This collection lives at the intersection between the dueling world-views of the book — "In Praise of Heart Attacks" and "In Fear of Heart Attacks." ... This book reminds me how grateful I am to be alive.

— Jennifer Franklin

CPSIA information can be obtained
at www.ICGtesting.com
Printed in the USA
BVHW041531020323
659560BV00008B/698